WHEN GREY GETS IN THE WAY

BLAKE LAWHON

PRISTINE
PRESS AND MEDIA

ISBN
978-1-964804-79-8 (Paperback)
978-1-964804-78-1 (eBook)
978-1-964804-80-4 (Hardcover)

ENDORSEMENTS

"When Grey Gets in the Way" is an eye opening book of self-discovery. Hope filled. Biblically energized. If your past is hindering your purpose; READ THIS BOOK. If you feel like there are forces against you; READ THIS BOOK. Your created purpose awaits."

—Dr. Robert Lewis
Pastor, Founder-Men's Fraternity

When I read *When Grey Gets in the Way* I feel like I'm in a pickup truck with the author, taking a riding on a long Texas high- way and catching the overflow of His awe-inspired wonder of a great God. "Grey" is a fun journey looking out of the window of that truck, at the starry night sky, at two kinds of light, natural light and the relationality of God, the highest revelation of God though Jesus Heb 1:1–3). The author brings his reader to understand the advan- tages of "night vision" that Jesus provides in the battle.

Lawhon, a compassionate guide, raises a series of illuminating questions in Chapter Three that have the power to bring daylight to the darkest places of our lives. Waiting for more to come.

—Dr. Kerry Wood
Author of "Gifts of the Spirit for a New
Generation" and "The Abba Trilogy"

"*When Grey Gets in the Way*" is a treasure that can deeply impact your faith. The inspirational true stories, practical life lessons and rich biblical insights will leave a lasting impact on all who read it!"

—Dave Willis
Pastor and bestselling author of "The Seven Laws of Love"

In this short, gentle, and often-entertaining work, Blake has given us fresh wisdom regarding spiritual light and darkness. *When Grey Gets in the Way* provides us with new insights into the nature of spiritual light and darkness from the analogy of physical light and darkness. But, above all, it provides us with much-needed awareness of the importance of avoiding any compromise with spiritual darkness in all its forms: falsehood, fear, bondage, and shame.

—Dr. Dan Lee
Author of *Life beyond Heaven: Where You Can Make Your Biggest Impact on Earth*

TABLE OF CONTENTS

ACKNOWLEDGEMENTS

Because this is my first book, I have no doubt that I will leave someone out here. Furthermore, I am quite positive at this point that I have been blindsided with favor throughout this entire process to the point where it will take years of reflection and revelation to know fully just who I should thank. That being said, there are several people I do want to mention.

I must start with my beautiful bride of twenty-six plus years.

Tracy, your support has never wavered. There are no words to express the depth of my love for you. Truly we are one. I must also say thank you for your proofing skills. They are, by far, the most impressive I have ever seen and you will be a part of all writing projects moving forward. I love you most.

To Shawna and Kyle Wortham, you were the first to pray over me at the beginning as I battled the thought of quitting my job to work on this project. Your appeal that morning has been met with comfort, peace, and so much confirmation through this process and I continue to carry your words of encouragement.

To Ariel Lawhon, my sis-in-law novelist extraordinaire, thank you for lending wisdom and experience as I attempted to make sense of the "writing a book" process. I owe you a few "off the ledge" talks. These challenges will not thwart our efforts.

To the staff at Northside Remedy, thank you for creating the greatest environment and the greatest chai lattes. Surely there must be an award for this.

To the greatest artist ever, Shane Scofield. I pray people look deep into the cover art. Your attention to detail is off the charts. To my Inner Circle for always covering me in prayer.

To Michael and Sherry for allowing me to experience Fresh Wind.

To Dan, you have been there from the beginning. I can't thank you enough for your friendship and belief in this process. Love you, bro.

And to my Lord and Savior, Jesus. This has truly been a great adventure. I pray this book does whatever You will it to do. Thank You for teaching me through this journey. Open their eyes so they may see Your love and goodness. You, indeed, are my light and salvation.

FOREWORD

B lake and I have been great friends for several years and he is always my 'go-to' guy for all things that relate to ministry. His heart for God and His Word is enormous and his heart for people is almost as big. It's a gift. I have learned so much about God, myself, and those around me as a result of spending many hours with him in a booth at Whataburger, on the golf course, or just in my office hanging out. He truly is a complementary ministry partner of mine. It reminds me of Paul and Silas in the New Testament and their partnership in ministry and how even through adversity, persecution, shipwrecks and imprisonment, they were still able to sing and rejoice in the Lord. I believe this to be our relationship. I truly love this guy!

As one of the Teaching Pastors of a multi-site church, I often times get a bird's-eye view of people as they develop into the calling that God has placed on them. Some may go from new believers to an apprenticeship within a certain area of leadership; others may be in a leadership role and are able to take their leadership to a higher level based on their capacity and calling. Blake is one of the latter people. He continues to hone his leadership skills, exercise his calling, and walk in his anointing. I see God unfurling him like a big sail on a ship, each layer He unfolds through the wind of His breath reveals more and more of His glory in him taking him to new and higher places.

What I appreciate the most about Blake is his ability to dive into Scripture and give you insight into the heart of God. He always has a unique way of looking at Scripture and what it might mean to us, how we can apply it to our lives, and ultimately what God is communicating to us, His people. His first response is often "What does God's Word say about it?" This is a question that comes from spending quality time in the presence of the Lord and continuing to draw from an eternal well that will always reveal, always satisfy, and never disappoint.

When Grey Gets in the Way is a wonderful picture of how God's glory is displayed through the light of the Holy Spirit in us, His creation, and how our humanity suffers when His glory is diminished in our lives through sin. Where I find most encouragement is Blake's liberal spreading of Scripture throughout the entire book, and how he applies it in such a colorful way to convey every point. What I love most is the comfort of knowing the Father of Light is always available to us, and we have victory over sin and death because of what He did for us on the cross. That is the best news we can ever hope for or imagine!

Well done,
Dan Rasmussen
Senior Pastor, Church for All Nations

INTRODUCTION

D arkness.
     It is where fear resides. And the enemy plays games. It was the landscape before the creation of the earth. And it harbors the anchors of shackles that hold so many of us in bondage. It is a place of torment, slavery, and shame. It is where the lies of life we all believe at some point live and powerfully reign.

The distinction between right and wrong, light and dark, brave and fearful seems obvious enough. One is good; one is not. One brings honor and edification; one brings trouble and strife. One is evidence of a truly free life; one is clearly not. And yet, if it's all so simple, so clear cut, *so obvious*, why is choosing the honorable, life-giving path sometimes beyond our ability to reason? After all, it's not just believers who can differentiate between right and wrong, light and dark.

Most of us, long before we had to adult, were taught the basics of good versus evil. Light meant goodness; darkness equaled evil. Even the world knows this to be understood. It's a universal understanding; not a litmus test of our spiritual depth. Movies, music, and literature give us ample proof of this 24/7.

But it's one thing to *know* it; it's entirely different to fully and completely *understand* the far-reaching impact this simple association brings with it. For those who read it, Scripture is full of examples and illustrations, stories and parables that give us ample explanation and encouragement throughout the story of all His creation.

But have you ever just stopped to ponder what all of this means? On a grand, universal scale? Or on a personal, every day context? Apart from studying the Bible, learning the stories, and practicing the commands, there are only so many questions we can definitively answer about our very existence.

Why us?

Why our grand design?

Where do the lines between free will and God-ordained direction intersect?

Existence, it seems, is a profound subject. I have always believed that everything—everything—was created for a purpose; otherwise there would be no necessity for the existence of anything at all. You can even make an argument for the pesky mosquito once you understand its most positive existence is to primarily serve as bird food. The jury is still out for me personally concerning skunks, but I'm sure there is some environmental, and hence spiritual, reason for their presence (of which I desire to learn from a distance).

> *The Lord has prepared everything for His purpose—*
> *even the wicked for the day of disaster. (Proverbs 16:4)*

That being said, the purpose of this book is to journey together as we investigate creation, separation, and the 'goulash of life,' otherwise known as *the grey areas*. There are as many grey areas as there are people's opinions on a specific subject. Beyond that, there are grey areas within the grey areas. There are shades of what some might consider agreeable; others not. There are conditions under which someone would find a situation acceptable; others not. And there are versions of almost universally accepted practices that some would be okay with; and still others not in the least. Grey is just the beginning.

Why do bad things happen to good people if God loves us so much? *Grey.*

How can some people so violently harm others? *Greyer.*

Why do we do things we know to be wrong? *Greyer still.*

The easy answer is the sinful nature of humanity. But to know more requires greater understanding—of human nature, of God's power, and the very messages for living found in Scripture.

I don't consider myself a writer, but rather a messenger of truth—*The Truth*. It is my hope throughout this book to explore and present the primary attributes of light and darkness, to align them with Scripture, and to present for discussion what God is try-

ing to teach each of us through His Word. In the following chapters, I will—

- investigate the reasons our Creator established absolute separation of light from darkness and why the two can't exist together;
- look at the power of light in both the physical and spiritual realm;
- examine some of the areas of darkness most likely to be hindering our relationships, health, and our ability to walk out, who we were created to be, and what we were created to do.

Our Creator desires for us to live out our purpose in freedom and with authority. But truth be told, this journey is far more difficult than it sounds. Issues arise, circumstances get personal, consequences loom all too close. Light and dark, good and evil—there are obvious preferences to be sure, but challenge steps in *When Grey Gets in the Way*.

My Story

I have experienced an undeserved portion of relational growth with the Father through the process of writing this book. I feel you need to know this as we proceed through this storyline. I have received several promptings from the Holy Spirit throughout this process, one of which is to tell the story of how this came to be. In fact, on October 16, 2017, at 11:15 p.m., I was prepared to go to sleep when I was suddenly overwhelmed as God gave me the sweetest kiss on the forehead, prompting me to recall our journey together and then this charge, "Write this as well."

It was so evident that my bride, Tracy, asked me if I was okay. I explained what had just occurred and that I needed to get up and make some notes. Please understand that as you read this account there are some scripture references. I encourage you to look these up

as they should allow for a greater picture of how the Father pursues us, teaches us, and loves us.

May 2016, 3:00 a.m.

God: "Hey, Blake, get up! Let's go for a walk."
(John 10:3–4)
Me: "It's dark."
God: "Is it?"
Me: "Here I am, Lord."
(Psalms 139:12)
God: "Take notes."
(Psalms 25:5)
Me: "I can't. It's dark."
God: "Is it?"
(Philippians 4:13)
Me: "I'll go. Thank you for wanting to spend time with me."
God: "You asked me to teach you."
Me: "But at 3:00 a.m.?"
God: "Remember when I took Saul's sight in order to transform him? In his time of despair, he quickly became the student. I can teach you great things as you rely more on me with minimal distractions. Do you trust Me?"
Me: "Yes, Father. Let's go."

For the next two hours, we walked and talked as He became the teacher and I the student. As my audience of one, He received my offering of worship and praise. He showed me things regarding His creation of light and why He had to immediately separate it from the darkness. He taught me about open doors with welcome mats and how we call them grey areas, where we invite deception in and mangle clarity. He used physical analogies of spiritual truths backed by Scripture to help me understand. It was an amazing start to a journey He began with me personally for greater understanding and advancement of His kingdom. I am still in awe of our time together that morning, in His presence, enlightened by His glory.

This became an increasing occurrence as my attention had been captured by Him. Among all of the chaos of life, the peace and intimacy

I was experiencing with the Father was so much more life-giving than physical rest. Psalms 30 proclaims that there is "joy in the morning," and I would have to agree. There have been times when He wakes me, prompting me to pray for certain people, which is in some ways ironic, but it has built my faith in ways I can't explain. I can only conclude that He does this to show His mercy and grace for others in the prompting for intercession. There are times He wants my worship, of which He is so worthy (even at 3:00 a.m.); and there are those times in the midst of life's uncomfortable circumstances when He knows I need comfort and He holds me as any good father would do for his child. He is the God of all comfort.

Fast forward to early August 2016, at 4:00 a.m.

God: "Hey, Blake, wake up!" **Me**: "Ha! You're late."
God: "Am I?"
God: "Let's go."
Me: "I'm waiting on you." (Isaiah 40:31)
Me: "Daddy, I really want to hear what You have for me this morning. My heart's desire is to just worship You for a while. Is that okay?" (1 Chronicles 16:23–31)
God: "Of course. I would like that."
Me: "I have so much to be thankful for. You have been so faithful. Please receive my offering of praise this morning."

During this time, what I poured out in worship was refilled in a way that can only be explained as filled to overflowing with revelation, understanding, and peace. I will never forget the next thing I heard, which is why we are here. In fact, I can remember the exact spot as I was stopped in my tracks.

5:17 a.m.

Me: "Say what?"

God: "You are going to write this."

Me: "This doesn't make

sense.

God: "My ways are not your ways.

(Isaiah 55:8)

Me: "I understand that and

I trust You, but You

created me to be logical. This is not logical at all."

God: "Blake, you have been faithful in what I have asked of you. I have told you this through many of my messengers. Just like in Habakkuk 2, this vision is for an appointed time. You will know the time as I reveal it to you. Until then, prepare yourself for the task. Posture to receive and I will pour out as you remain obedient."

Me: "Is it okay that I am excited and scared at the same time?"

God: "Excited and expectant, yes, but fear is not from me. I am for you. I am calling you to walk in confidence. Anything else is grey, and you know that grey impedes purpose. As for logic, Jesus defied logic at the cross. He is why we are talking today."

Me: "I trust You. I have so many 'buts,' however I know those are just elements of a lack of faith. Father, help my unbelief. I surrender all."

(Mark 9:24)

God: "Faithful one, do you remember the word I gave you for 2016?"

Me: "Yes, walk."

God: "And…"

Me: "You have shown Your faithfulness as I choose to walk in obedience."

God: "YES, I gave that to you for this very moment. Remember where this started with a walk."

Me: "Of course."

God: "You have so many questions, but I am faithful and trust-worthy. My word will guide you when you don't have answers. It is a light for your path."

(Psalms 119:105)

The next six months can only be equated to one of the most intense battles I have ever faced because it was a spiritual battle that manifested itself mentally. One of my major life struggles (like many) has been the approval of man. I know that daily I must choose who I serve and what I believe, but the internal dialogue was deafening. I'm not an author. I didn't have time to do this and everything else I was already committed to. How was I supposed to do this and serve in the other capacities I have been called to? The questions were endless until the Holy Spirit whispered, "Remember."

That's because back in 2007, the Holy Spirit told me that I would be in full time ministry *unpaid*. I was reminded that part of Holy Spirit's ministry is to tell us what is to come as we are able to receive it. And now, as I write this, I am reminded that this information was given to me after I had been part of a downsizing and at the height of my professional career. Hindsight has truly proven to be 20/20 and every day I trust Him more.

> *I am amazed that you are so quickly turning away*
> *from Him who called you by the grace of Christ and are*
> *turning to a different gospel—not that there is another*
> *gospel, but there are some who are troubling you and want*
> *to change the good news about the Messiah.*

But even if we or an angel from heaven should preach to you a gospel other than what we have preached to you, a curse be on him! As we have said before, I now say again: if anyone preaches to you a gospel contrary to what you received, a curse be on him!

For am I now trying to win the favor of people, or God? Or am I striving to please people? If I were still trying to please people, I would not be a slave of Christ. (Galatians 1:6–10)

All of this was pointing me to leave the corporate workforce and give my time away to write this book. But again, my logical side battled with my faith in the One who has always proven Himself to me. My heart's desire was to be obedient, but my flesh continued to delay. It was much like a father encouraging his child to jump off the diving board for the first time. All the while my Father had created a safe platform as He encouraged me to launch into something I had never done before. And the promise He gave me? A new depth of freedom, a new way of living that was full of great expectations and blessings. It was such a gentle and patient time that gave me a new perspective on being a father.

Father: "Jump, son."

Me: "I want to, but I can't."

Father: "You can do ALL things through Christ who gives you strength."

Me: "I know, but it doesn't make sense."

Father: "Hmmm, this conversation is very familiar."

Me: "I know! Please see my heart."

Father: "I do."

(1 Samuel 16:7)

Me: "What about...?"

Father: "It's gonna be great."

Me: "I know, but..."

Father: "It's all taken care of."

Me: "I need my father's blessing."

Father: "Go get it."

Father: "When you are ready to jump, I am here."

Me: "Your love is amazing. Thank You for always teaching me."

Father: "You should see what I see. My plans for you will unfold as you act within your faith. Continue to seek me."

(Jeremiah 29:11–13)

Me: "Thank you, Father."

During this time, the Father gently walked me through mental struggles, personal doubts, and lots of questions. And each time, He brought comfort to my soul in so many ways. I asked many close prayer warriors to pray over and for me and had many speak words of comfort over me. The Holy Spirit counseled me and gave me just enough vision to take the steps of obedience to the call He had given me. There was no doubt throughout this process that Scripture is unequivocally true. Just as He did for me, He will do for *you*. God will make a way while He molds each of us into the likeness of His Son, Jesus.

> *This is what the Lord says—who makes a way in the sea, and a path through surging waters, who brings out the chariot and horse, the army and the mighty one together (they lie down, they do not rise again; they are extinguished, quenched like a wick)—Do not remember*

the past events, pay no attention to the things of old. Look, I am about to do something new; even now it is coming. Do you not see it? Indeed, I will make a way in the wilderness, rivers in the desert. (Isaiah 43:16–19)

So then, my dear friends, just as you have always obeyed, not only in my presence, but now even more in my absence, work out your own salvation with fear and trembling. For it is God who is working in you, enabling you both to will and to act for His good purpose. (Philippians 2:12–14)

CHAPTER 1

LIGHT'S CREATION

The creation story has always amazed me; I never get tired of reading it. Why did the Lord create man in the first place? I mean, really, what could we bring to the table that He didn't already have or know? Nothing. Absolutely nothing.

Think about it. Imagine yourself all powerful and all knowing. You exist and communicate in triplicate—as Father, as Son, and Holy Spirit. What could possibly be lacking?

Relationship.

God desired relationship. But not just any relationship; He wanted relationship with His own creation. Throughout Scripture, it is overwhelmingly obvious that God desired connection and communion with those crafted in His own image. But why? Consider the desires a good father holds dearest for his children—to grow and lead them into maturity and beyond. Isn't that precisely what God wants for each of His children? And Jesus? As the Savior of mankind willing to go the distance, He required a beneficiary for His ultimate sacrifice. As for the Holy Spirit, His hope was in someone to counsel, guide, convict, and speak of things to come. The takeaway? God didn't *need* us; He *desired* community with us.

> *Then God said, "Let Us make man in Our image, according to Our likeness." (Genesis 1:26a)*

Consider for a moment the magnitude of this verse. We—you, me, your bothersome brother-in-law, the checker at the grocery store, *everyone*—we were created *in His* likeness; to have His attributes, and to be relational *with Him*. Kind of takes your breath away, doesn't it?

After speaking the heavens, the earth, and beyond *all* into being, God surveyed His creation. The very first area He sought to correct—man's loneliness.

> *Then the Lord God said, "It is not good for the*
> *man to be alone. I will make a helper who is like him."*
> *(Genesis 2:18)*

God wanted connection between himself and man and he wanted man to have connection, one to another. Community is God's creation and our desire for it is God-breathed. We were created to long for community with Him and one another.

Skeptics of the creation story have worked for centuries to poke holes in the congruency of the details. Is Genesis a literal account or is it a more figurative retelling? And what about the days—was a day as we have come to know it or was it untold eons yet to be defined by man? And what was the source of the light attributed to Day One's creation if the sun, the moon, and the stars weren't created until the fourth day?

For me, I imagine the conversation between God, the Holy Spirit, and Jesus went something like this:

Holy Spirit: "It is really dark over this earth and quiet. You have been pondering Your creation, but where do We start?"

God: "Let there be light."

Jesus: "And you want me to do what? Talk about the short straw. But I'll do it because I love them."

If you consider the Bible to be infallible, how can you explain these gaps in clarity and points that seem to contradict one another? It takes a bit of investigative research and moving beyond merely relying upon an English translation, but therein lies the answer. I had so many questions when I first started this book, but the insights I've gained from returning to original translations have completely changed the way I read the Bible.

When I ventured into the land of Hebrew texts, I discovered something fascinating: there are actually two words, with two different meanings, that both translate into 'light' in the English language. I also came to realize the tremendous significance we can sometimes lose in translation moving from an original text to English. The difference can be enough to alter a verse's true intended meaning. Whether translated from Greek, Hebrew, or Aramaic, both the Old and New Testament are occasionally compromised when written in English. As complex as the English language is to master, when applied to Biblical translation, it really is a simplified version of the original text. I promise you, a word study referencing Hebrew and/or Greek origins of major biblical themes can be incredibly insightful.

Our study of the word *light* will make this point. Follow along:

> *Then God said, "Let there be light," and there was light. God saw that the light was good. (Genesis 1:3–4a)*

According to Torahclass.com, the Hebrew word for 'light' in Genesis 1:3–4 is *aur*, pronounced "owr."[1] It is singular and means illumination and enlightenment and is closely associated with life, joy, and good. This light carries a dual reality in that it has both physical and spiritual qualities. It is a light that is required to sustain life and a light that will never die. It is an *eternal light*.

> *Then God said, "Let there be lights in the expanse of the sky to separate the day from the night. They will serve as signs for festivals and for days and years. They will be lights in the expanse of the sky to provide light on the earth." (Genesis 1:14–15)*

In *these* verses, the word used for light is *marth*, pronounced "maorot." In this sense, this word refers to an object that emits light and is only physical in nature and is intended to excite the eyes of humans and animals.[2] Clearly, the lights these refer to are the sun, the moon, and the stars. And while it is hard to imagine the earth void of these lights, we are promised in Revelation there will come a time when they will cease to shine.

Night will no longer exist, and people will not need lamplight or sunlight, because the Lord God will give them light. And they will reign forever and ever. (Revelation 22:5)

So far, we've discovered two distinct meanings of light, all within the first chapter of the first book of the Bible. Yet still the question remains: what was the source of light three full days before the introduction of the sun, the moon, and the stars. Though hard to definitively describe, this 'God-sourced' light is present not only 'in the beginning,' but is also present numerous times throughout Scripture. Some theologians describe this mysterious light as "the primordial essence of God, or God's Shekinah Glory."[3]

The disciple John makes a glorious reference to the supernatural, transcendent nature of God in 1 John:

God is light; in Him there is no darkness at all. (1 John 5:9)

The prophet Isaiah prophesied of this great light and the context of this prophecy was fulfilled right before Jesus chose His first disciples in the Book of Matthew:

The people walking in darkness have seen a great light on those living in the land of darkness, a light has dawned. (Isaiah 9:2)

The people who live in darkness have seen a great light and for those living in the shadowland of death, light has dawned. (Matthew 4:16)

See the amazing similarity between prophesy and fulfillment? Light was foretold and light was presented.

More than a few people have made the parallel to the center of our physical universe, the sun, and the center of our spiritual universe as Christians, *the Son*. Just as the sun provides warmth, comfort, and most importantly, light, so also does *The Son* of Man. The difference between the two lies in semantics. The sun *emits* light; Jesus *is* the light. Jesus, being fully God and fully man, carried the light of the Father in His person.

> *Then Jesus spoke to them again: "I am the light of*
> *the world. Anyone who follows Me will never walk in the*
> *darkness but will have the light of life. (John 8:12)*

This light of life is written about in the first chapter of John, describing Jesus as The Living Word.

> *Life was in Him, and that life was the light of men.*
> *That light shines in the darkness, yet the darkness did not*
> *overcome it. (John 1:4–5)*

Both of these verses share the same clear similarities regarding Jesus—his illuminating presence and his victory over darkness. What might not be so obvious, but is strongly implied, is that this light— *His light*—was and continues to be intended to be shared and passed on to others for their benefit. It is something akin to a 'bear it and share it' mindset.

The significance of Jesus as a supernatural source of light cannot be overstated. There are no comparable others. He is *the one, the only* source of eternity-giving light and life. He shared His holy charge— to carry and share His light with all who would come after Him—in the most famous of his teachings, the Sermon on the Mount:

> *You are the light of the world. A city situated on a hill*
> *cannot be hidden. No one lights a lamp and puts it under*
> *a basket, but rather on a lamp stand, and it gives light for*
> *all who are in the house.*

> *In the same way, let your light shine before men, so that*
> *they may see your good works and give glory to your Father*
> *in heaven. (Matthew 5:14–16)*

This light of salvation Jesus refers to is strong. It is unflinching. It is *radiant*. It is meant to send out or emit light, to shine, or to glow brightly. There is a reason Scripture says "let your light shine" and that is to set us apart as believers. We are to be so extraordinarily filled with Christ's presence that others can't help but take note and ask why.

These verses bring to my mind something we can all relate to: traffic. Virtually every time I drive at night, someone in oncoming traffic has their high-beams on. Sure, they're bothersome and best used on isolated stretches, but you know what? They get our attention because they're different and they give off such a bright light, you can't help but notice.

Interestingly, our usual first response is to flash our lights at them as a corrective measure. We want them to dim their lights so that they better align with the norm. Sadly, that's not much different than what we do in life as well. When we operate in our 'grey areas,' our light is dimmed and we're brought more in line with what society wants, not what Jesus commands. We concede and want others to do the same. This pull of the world and our need for community and acceptance can dim even the brightest lights of conviction at different times throughout our lives. Sometimes we're the influenced, sometimes the influencer. Or sometimes the conformer, sometimes the catalyst. It can happen when we're twelve, thirty-three, or sixty-five.

Mackenzie's Story

My kids are probably pretty much like yours. Loved, valued, and more than just a bit imperfect. Still, each of them has in their own way given me and my wife so, so many reasons to be proud of them as they've worked to discover who they were created to be and what they are called to do.

My middle daughter, Mackenzie, is a fifteen-year-old determined follower of Jesus. She is beautiful, vibrant, and has a zest for life like no one I have ever seen. She is magnetic in her presence and loves everyone. She can have a quality conversation with anyone from one to one hundred and then leave them smiling. This is probably why so many of her peers often feel comfortable sharing their personal problems with her. She is a stunning example of a true friend.

She also has an incredible vocal talent and musical anointing and has been leading worship at our church since she was thirteen years old—no small feat for a young teenage girl. Most of the time, when she enters a room she so brightly shines the light of Christ that others can't help but be drawn to her. She works diligently and intentionally to maintain an integrity beyond reproach.

Because Mackenzie is involved in leadership at the church and stays tremendously busy, my wife and I make an effort to remind her to just be a kid sometimes. Hang out with your friends. Go to the movie. Head to the football game.

But here's the catch: because her peers know that she is different by her presence, she is frequently left out of the usual teenage get-to-gethers—the parties, the birthdays, just the casual meet-ups at the mall. And on several of the times when she has been included, there have been moments her faith was challenged by some very uncomfortable situations. We've helped her with a few exit strategies when she finds herself in these 'grey areas,' but that eventually leads her to feel isolated, alone, and left out of what all her peers are enjoying. As a parent, it breaks my heart to see my child hurting. We've told her that leadership can be extremely lonely and while she understands, the loneliness sometimes remains. For Mackenzie, worship recharges and refuels her like nothing else of the world. It is a beautiful thing to watch her light go from dim to radiant in song and praise.

Recently, it was brought to her attention that an acquaintance had begun spreading rumors. And not just trivial comments in passing; some really horrible lies. Several of her friends brought this information to my daughter because they knew them to be false, but wanted her to know. Mackenzie was at a crossroads: she could allow the comments to dim her radiance and bring her down to the norm and react as her flesh would want or she could follow the scriptural teaching deep in her spirit and walk away. I am proud to say she chose the latter. As we talked through the hurt she said, "You always tell us to not repay evil for evil." I have to admit, it made for a proud parent moment.

We teach our children that truth will always prevail and light will always thwart the secret activities of darkness and exposes its lies and tactics.

> *Truthful lips endure forever, but a lying tongue, only a moment. (Proverbs 12:19)*

All of this has caused me to deeply evaluate how I signal others to correct or dim their lights when I'm met with their oncoming brightness.

The total solar eclipse of August 2017 makes an awesome illustration of this truth. Even though by definition, a total eclipse means the sun is completely covered by the moon, it's still not safe to view with an unprotected human eye. There are precautions to take and equipment to use to properly and safely see the eclipse. And here's the irony of it all—the sun's power is not diminished even when it is covered up. The light that does come through, though mostly covered by the moon, is just as strong as ever. It is just as bright. It is just as damaging to the unprotected eye. And it is terrific proof that even something as enormous as the moon cannot stop the sun's light from reaching us. Darkness, be it physical or spiritual, will never have victory over light.

Reflecting on the eclipse, I often wonder about the glory of God. The magnitude, the detailed precision, the singular plan for each of us is more than just a bit overwhelming. In Exodus 33, Moses asked to see God's glory. He had been in fellowship face to face with Him for a time and felt comfortable asking. However, to make this possible, God had to produce a cloud in order to protect Moses from the blinding radiance of these encounters.

In this story, God provided even more protection. He placed Moses upon a rock as He passed by. But beyond that, He put Moses in the rock's crevice and placed His hand over him for extra protection. As He passed, He allowed Moses to see His back, but not His face, because He knew the radiance would have been too much and meant death for Moses.

Saul's encounter on the road to Damascus in Acts 9 brings to mind another example of God's transformational light. On a routine journey to persecute followers of "The Way," Saul is on the roadside and suddenly blinded by an intense light. Because I believe this blinding light to be the glorified Jesus, it is no wonder it left Saul in complete darkness and unable to overcome the light. Saul endured three full days of complete darkness for one simple reason: to fully understand the radical transformation of his heart *away* from God, *toward* God.

I have always enjoyed stargazing. The masterful creation of the Milky Way galaxy is literally beyond comprehension to even the most astute astronomers. Because I grew up in the city where city lights made it difficult to enjoy the full beauty of the heavens, I've become very intentional in looking for opportunities to escape the city limits and watch the nighttime skies come to life. Several years back I took my family to Fort Davis, Texas. And while the telescopes were pretty amazing, what I found most interesting in the immense darkness were the stars; they actually felt close enough to reach out and grab. The light of these stars shone brightest in the darkest of skies. I've heard it said that darkness is nothing more than the absence of light, but I believe the opposite is true as well. Light, in its truest existence, is the absence of darkness.

> *Long ago God spoke to the fathers by the prophets at different times and in different ways.*
> *In these last days, He has spoken to us by His Son, whom He has appointed heir of all things and through whom He made the universe.*
> *He is the radiance of His glory, the exact expression of His nature, and He sustains all things by His powerful word.*
> *After making purification for sins, He sat down at the right hand of the Majesty on high. (Hebrews 1:1–3)*

The life and ministry of Jesus were exactly like that. Contrary to the teachings and judgment of the Pharisees and religious leaders, Jesus went to the places where there was no light to impact and love others. He went beyond the city gates to spend time with the outcasts, the diseased, the possessed, the beggars, and the hopeless— what He deemed "the least of these." Jesus had no boundaries then and doesn't today.

Jesus made clear His expectations for each of us and what we are to do with the love of His light.

> *I give you a new command: Love one another. Just as*
> *I have loved you, you must also love one another.*
> *By this all people will know you are My disciples, If you*
> *have love for one another. (John 13:34–35)*

When we remember the promise of Scripture that darkness will not overcome light, we have to consider the Gospel of Truth. This eternal light was not snuffed out when Jesus was crucified on the cross and placed in the tomb. Nor was it dimmed over the next three days as Jesus defeated death and took His light forward—into the heart of darkness. This victory—this triumph of light over dark—is the victory we claim in His resurrection.

Let's return for a moment to the investigation of *aur*, the light that represents the very presence of God and how it relates to the Holy Spirit. In John, Chapter 14, Jesus tells the disciples about "The Counselor" who is coming and that he is the Spirit of Truth. As God is also the Holy Spirit, the third person of the Trinity, it follows that He should also carry this light. In John, Chapter 16, Jesus explained to the disciples the ministry of the Holy Spirit:

> *When He comes, He will convict the world about sin,*
> *righteousness, and judgment. (John 16:8)*
> *When the Spirit of truth comes, He will guide you into*
> *all the truth. For He will not speak on His own, but He*
> *will speak whatever He hears. He will also declare to you*
> *what is to come. (John 16:13)*

It's clear—the Holy Spirit is equally empowered to be the light that guides our daily lives. He is available to us as followers of Christ to guide us "into all the truth." He will not force Himself upon anyone, but stands readily available to bring light and truth to our everyday battles and to help us develop a battle plan for our lives.

> *For our battle is not against flesh and blood, but against*
> *the rulers, against the authorities, against the world powers*
> *of this darkness, against the spiritual forces of evil in the*
> *heavens. (Ephesians 6:12)*

Because so many of our daily battles exist in the spiritual realm, we are not always able to see the prevailing darkness. Make no mistake—it is most certainly present, just not always visible. We are in desperate need of a guide, a director, a counselor to light the path before us. Having been battle tested from the beginning, our Holy Spirit is worthy of the rank of Commanding General of our lives. But again, He will only answer our request for help and will not interfere uninvited. It is almost as if the light He carries can be compared to the 'night vision' of our lives because He helps us see through the darkness. It's not surprising then, that the value our service men and women place on having highly developed night vision skills and equipment is immense and *lifesaving*.

Here are two responses by actual Marines to this question:

What one thing gives you the greatest advantage in the darkness from a military standpoint? Intelligence, better weapons, stealth capability, radar, or night vision?

> *Being comfortable at night with nothing will always*
> *give you the greatest advantage. It is unnatural for humans*
> *to hunt and operate in the dead of night. If you become*
> *used to this and comfortable with no night vision, then*
> *you will almost always be better with it. This is the reason*
> *spec ops guys do a majority of their training at night.*
> *Most people are uncomfortable in the dark, and when your*
> *enemy is losing sleep because you come out of the shadows,*

their combat power is degraded through fatigue. This is true on both a small unit and large unit scale. (Corporal Travis P. Yandell, United States Marine Corps)

I have been a pilot since 2001, flying the CH-53E, deploying four times. I was an instructor at the Marine Corps Aviation Weapons School and a night system instructor flying over half my hours at night. I currently serve as the Heavy Helicopter Requirements Officer, Headquarters Marine Corps for Deputy Commandant for Aviation in the Pentagon. I have been selected as the Commanding Officer Marine Heavy Helicopter Squadron 464, where I will take Command next year.

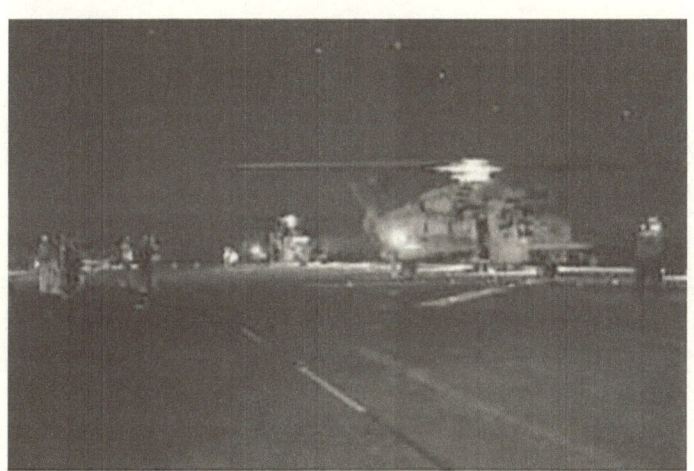

While flying in the dark, the military utilizes multiple tools and equipment in order to gain the advantage over the enemy. Nothing in the arsenal gains us more advantage than night vision, especially while flying. Without night vision, we are not only fighting the enemy, but fighting uncertainty due to lack of vision. As Christians, we often try to navigate the darkness and try to use what we have at our own disposal, instead of first trusting the Holy Spirit to provide us the greatest advantage while flying in the dark. Because we have the Holy Spirit providing our vision

during spiritual warfare, we can be sure that we are in the best position to defeat the enemy. Night Vision Devices take a source of light and amplify it. Night Vision Goggles utilize moonlight, starlight, auroras, and air glow, magnifying the light, providing vision. In the dark, light always exists, it just takes the Holy Spirit to magnify the light when we don't think we see it. (Lt. Colonel Tom Trimble, United States Marine Corps)

It is important that we understand that our comfort is given to us in the knowledge of who we are in Christ and our identity as followers of Him. Being a son or daughter of the Most High God makes us heirs in the kingdom of God.

> *All those led by God's Spirit are God's sons. For you did not receive a spirit of slavery to fall back into fear, but you received the Spirit of adoption, by whom we cry out, "Abba, Father!" The Spirit Himself testifies together with our spirit that we are*
> *God's children, And if children, also heirs—heirs of God and co-heirs with Christ—Seeing that we suffer with Him so that we may also be glorified with Him. (Romans 8:14–17)*

But this gift of salvation, eternity, and fellowship with the Most Holy One, though free, does not come without expectations. This is how Jesus explained it:

> *Much will be required of everyone who has been given much. And even more will be expected of the one who has been entrusted with more. (Luke 12:48)*

As believers, we are called to be responsible in our daily lives and to live according to Scripture's instruction and wisdom. Even in our comfort, it is necessary that we realize the advantage we have in the Holy Spirit and the power He holds to enlighten us with truth as we face spiritual trials.

Besides the powerful words of Scripture, we also have at our disposal the ongoing comfort of prayer and the support and fellowship of other believers. The presence, accountability, and encouragement we can offer one believer to another benefits us individually and strengthens the entire body of Christ. Our shared faith gives us hope and deepens our relationships with one another.

> *Iron sharpens iron, and one man sharpens another.*
> *(Proverbs 27:17)*

Now that we have a better understanding about light—who has it, where it comes from, and what it does, we can begin understanding why light had to be separated from darkness.

CHAPTER 2

PURPOSEFUL SEPARATION

Most of us as children remember growing up and feeling very uncomfortable, even scared, if we became separated from our parents. Our security was gone and we were apart from the relationship that mattered most to us at the time. We were born with a need for relationships from the start.

As a small child, I can remember many times after I was put to bed for the night I would sneak back out and lay on the floor just out of sight from my parents. There was safety there, and I didn't want to miss anything. If I wasn't caught, I would just fall asleep on the floor. It wasn't that I was afraid of being alone; it's just that I didn't want to be. Even worse than that, was being confined to the dark, in the imagined dungeon which was my room.

As a child, there is so much unknown to us. And with this vast unknown oftentimes come fear. Is there a monster under my bed? Did that stuffed clown just move? If I go to sleep, is the clown going to get my family? It sounds silly now, but for a kid, the fear is genuine.

As mature believers, however, fear has no place in our belief system. In fact, we're told specifically not to fear, not to worry, or not to doubt that anything is beyond God including the clown in the corner.

> *Don't worry about anything, but in everything, through prayer and petition with thanksgiving, let your request be made known to God. And the peace of God, which surpasses every thought, will guard your hearts and your minds in Christ Jesus. (Philippians 4:6–7)*

And again, we're encouraged in 2 Timothy:

God did not give us a spirit of fear, but one of power,
love, and sound judgment. (2 Timothy 1:17)

Fear is a byproduct of the darkness. Nothing of God brings with it fear because God is able to do all things, in all ways, in all circumstances. In the beginning, when darkness covered the surface of the watery depths, I can only imagine that God knew darkness would not be a good and healthy environment for His creation and even more so for His children. God, just like any loving parent, created a place of peace and protection for each of us as we move into His presence.

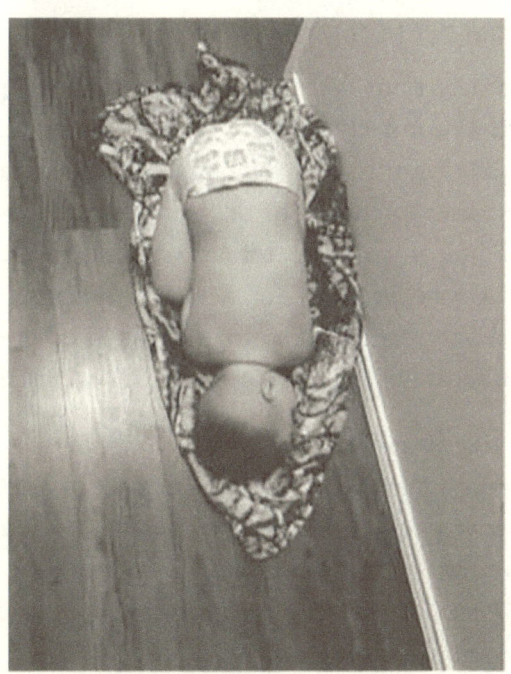

In our world today, things are much different than they were forty years ago when I was a kid. We used to play anywhere in our neighborhood as long as we were home before dinner. Now it seems as if evil has broadened its reach as the powers of darkness have slowly encroached upon freedom's territory. No more cap guns, cowboys and Indians, or even playing outside the perimeter of the front yard. Even wearing a certain color has been driven to a point of endangerment. It can even seem as if darkness has us backed into a corner at times.

As a parent, I am charged as being the protector of my children. Because of this, it's my job to be vigilant for teaching opportunities to pour the truth into my children. Some of these opportunities involve helping my children learn to identify darkness and to recognize its craftiness.

In creating light to represent good and darkness to stand for evil, the Lord created two distinct and symbolic settings to allow us to better navigate the world we live in. And He did so in the very beginning:

> *God saw that the light was good, and God separated the light from the darkness. (Genesis 1:4)*

According to Merriam-Webster, the definition of separated is a) to set or keep apart: disconnect or sever, b) to make a distinction between: discriminate or distinguish. The archaic definition means to set aside for a special purpose, to choose or dedicate.[4] Knowing this, it speaks volumes that God separated light from the darkness instead of darkness from light. Light was set apart for a special purpose. What's more, light and dark simply cannot exist together in the same space. If one is present, the other is absent and vice versa. It's an either/or decision.

> *Do not be mismatched with unbelievers. For what partnership is there between righteousness and lawlessness? Or what fellowship does light have with darkness? Therefore, come out from among them and be separate, says the Lord; do not touch any unclean thing, and I will welcome you. (2 Corinthians 6:14, 17)*
>
> *The one who walks with the wise will become wise, but a companion of fools will suffer harm. (Proverbs 13:20)*

Just as the word light has two meanings, so also does the word darkness. According to Torahclass.com, the Hebrew word for darkness is *"choshek"* and it is used as the opposite of *"aur."* Embodied in *choshek* is the sense of blindness, misery, and ignorance, leading to death and destruction. Unlike the Hebrew word for night (*layil*), which is just the opposite of day, *choshek* has spiritually evil overtones and is negative in nature.[5] Just understanding this slight but important difference can help us to better understand Scripture.

Now that we've established light from dark, the kinds of light and dark, and the source of all light as God, who is the head of all the darkness? Scripture has many names for him—Satan, the enemy, the devil, Lucifer, the tempter, accuser of the brethren, the adversary, liar, the serpent, prince of the darkness, thief, a wolf in sheep's clothing, and many others. Of all the names used to identify the source of darkness, none are good.

Here are just a few of the references to the nature of the ruler of the dark:

> *A thief comes only to steal and to kill and to destroy. I have come that they may have life and have it in abundance. (John 10:10)*
>
> *Be sober! Be on the alert! Your adversary the devil is prowling around like a roaring lion, looking for anyone he can devour. (1 Peter 5:8)*
>
> *Now the serpent was the most cunning of all the wild animals that the Lord God had made. He said to the woman, "Did God really say, 'You can't eat from any tree in the garden?'" (Genesis 3:1)*
>
> *And no wonder! For Satan himself is disguised as an angel of light. So it is no great thing if his servants also disguise themselves as servants of righteousness. Their destiny will be according to their works. (2 Corinthians 11:14–15)*
>
> *You are of your father, the Devil, and you want to carry out your father's desires.*
>
> *He was a murderer from the beginning and has not stood in the truth, because there is no truth in him.*
>
> *When he tells a lie, he speaks from his own nature, because he is a liar and the father of lies. (John 8:44)*

Satan had, and continues to have, one thing on his mind: destruction of all that God had made. In the beginning, he wanted nothing more than to undo the beauty of creation. Today, his focus remains the same—to kill, steal, and destroy Christ's presence in our lives. That's why it is so important to see that what we call 'grey areas' are simply examples of his craftiness, which he uses to deceive and mislead us into granting him access into our lives. Once allowed in, darkness gains a foothold and Satan gets about the business—*his business*—as he seeks to kill, steal, and destroy our reliance on Christ.

Our battle with darkness goes back to the beginning of man. As long as man has been given free will over his life, Satan has been busy setting traps. God, however, punished both serpent and man for their moments of darkness:

> *Then the Lord God said to the serpent: Because you have done this, you are cursed more than any livestock and more than any wild animal. You will move on your belly and eat **dust** all the days of your life. (Genesis 3:14)*
>
> *To Adam: You will eat bread by the sweat of your brow until you return to the ground, since you were taken from it. For you are **dust**, and you will return to **dust**. (Genesis 3:19)*

The devil is after all of us. You. Me. *Everyone.* If you take a few moments of self-evaluation, there is a good chance you can easily identify some places he is currently staking claim in your life. There is also a good chance that he is telling you to put this book down or toss it away. But don't. Remember, there is no truth in him. If he is speaking, he is lying. Ever since his deception of Eve, he has not stopped scheming, plotting, and planning for the demise of Christfollowers. The battle of light vs. dark, of God vs. Satan, is a real battle inside each of us.

> *For our battle is not against flesh and blood, but against the rulers, against the authorities, against the world powers of this darkness, against the spiritual forces of evil in the heavens. (Ephesians 6:12)*

In this verse, we can see that in darkness authority has been given. We can also see by the plural references that there is not just one source of evil, but possibly many. Though the numbers are unknown, it could be said that Satan holds court over all things evil and could be suitably referred to as the Chief Destructive Officer.

Regarding the physical and scientific differentiators between light and darkness, some are significant; others not so much. Some are clearly understood while others remain a mystery. And some are completely objective and some considered purely subjective.

The Masters Golf Tournament is a great example of these principles of light and darkness. It is probably the most prestigious golf tournament on the PGA tour. What makes it such an honor to win is the challenge of the course at Augusta National Golf Club. The course is challenging in its own right, but as the light of the sun retreats toward the west and every blade of grass follows, shadows loom from every direction making it increasingly difficult to navigate the ominous greens. If you have watched this tournament in the past, you know what I am referring to. There are definite advantages to playing earlier in the day before the sun begins its descent. As created, even the laws of nature instruct the plants to follow the light of the sun.

Once the shadows begin to set in, the undulation of the greens are extremely hard to see with the human eye. In the game of golf, the other players are your opponents but not your enemy; the course is the real enemy. And so it follows, that on a course like Augusta, it is vital that you study your enemy and get to know every sand trap, fairway, putting green, and water hazard if you intend to better your opponents' scores. As a player, you must be aware of what awaits you once the shadows begin to creep into view.

This leads me to better understand one of the most important characteristics of darkness—that it is a slow operator, sneaky and deceptive in every way. Darkness is always attempting to call each of us into a destructive decision. The prince of darkness is relentless— always on the prowl, always seeking signs of weakness and potential for compromise.

Light, on the other hand, travels at 186,000 miles per second. It permeates the darkness wherever it is granted access. This usually takes a submissive action such as closing an umbrella, opening a cellar, or uncovering something hidden. In the open, you cannot escape light; it will always find you and truth will be revealed.

> *Every generous act and every perfect gift is from above,*
> *coming down from the Father of lights; with Him there is*
> *no variation or shadow cast by turning. (James 1:17)*

What this means is simple: truth is constant and does not change based on our opinions, environments, or circumstances. Truth is trustworthy, not subject to outside influences. That being said, what we call 'half-truths' only exist within the false realities or fantasy lands we are deceived into believing in.

There is a reason why there is no peace walking down a dark alley. (For the record, I DO NOT suggest ever doing that.) Our common sense triggers our anxiety; the anxiety is fueled by fear, and we know fear is not from God and therefore not a good idea. Figuratively, we face dark alleys every day. And every day we must ask ourselves, "What is my dark alley?" and "What is hiding there that is fearful to me?" and "What have I hidden away in the darkness to save myself from shame and embarrassment?"

> *Now this is the message we have heard from Him*
> *and declare to you: God is light, and there is absolutely no*
> *darkness in Him.*
> *If we say, "We have fellowship with Him," and walk*
> *in darkness, we are lying and are not practicing the truth.*
> *But if we walk in the light, as He Himself is in the*
> *light, we have fellowship with one another, and the blood*
> *of Jesus His Son cleanses us from all sin.*

If we say, "We have no sin," we are deceiving ourselves, and the truth is not in us. (1 John 1:5–8)

CHAPTER 3

DARK ALLEYS-
DOORWAYS, SHADOWS,
AND DUMPSTERS

Both The Man And His Wife WereNaked, Yet Felt No Shame. (Genesis 2:25)

This was the original design of the Father's creation. He wanted nothing more than for us to live in perfect peace and close community with Him. There was to be no guilt, no shame, and no secrets because there was nothing to hide. There were rules, however, that were necessary to not only keep Adam and Eve in right standing with God, but also to provide guidance and protect their ability to remain in relationship with God.

Apart from Him and by offering the one rule He gave Adam and Eve, He was calling them to obedience for their own good. Their instruction from the Lord was simple:

> *You are free to eat from any tree of the garden, but you must not eat from the tree of the knowledge of good and evil. (Genesis 2:16)*

I can only imagine how beautiful the Garden of Eden was knowing that sin had not yet entered the human DNA. The fruit had to be outstanding, perfect in every way. And then Satan arrives. Disguised as the serpent, he came ready to kill, steal, and destroy God's perfection. By questioning the Lord's instruction, Satan planted the seed of doubt and was able to deceive first Eve, then Adam, by channeling their curiosity into disobedience. It worked then and it still works today. We doubt; we break communion with God, and then we hide in our guilt and shame.

> *Then the eyes of both of them were opened, and they knew they were naked; so they sewed fig leaves together and made loincloths for themselves.*
>
> *Then the man and his wife heard the sound of the Lord God walking in the garden at the time of the evening breeze, and they hid themselves from the Lord God among the trees of the garden.*
>
> *So the Lord God called out to the man and said to him, "Where are you?"*
>
> *And he said, "I heard you in the garden, and I was afraid because I was naked, so I hid." (Genesis 3:7–10)*

I can remember as a child the many times my parents gave me instruction calling me to obedience and the many times I defied their oversight. I recall the pain in the pit of my stomach reminding me of the wrong I had done and the thoughts I would have as I wondered how to cover up or hide my rebellion. We all know the feeling of disobedience; no one escaped childhood without testing the limits of obedience.

Just like Adam and Eve, for most of us our initial response to disobedience is to feel guilt and shame right after we do wrong. We know when we've done wrong and the devil is the accuser that will forever remind you of your wrongdoing. He will lie to you about the guilt and shame you should feel and the necessity to hide this sin away. He will also deceive you by warping truth and by supporting you in your futile self-justification, usually using your circumstances as the reason you sinned. "If this hadn't happened, I wouldn't have done *that*." "I wouldn't have gone there if you had stopped me." "I wasn't hurting anyone. The opportunity presented itself and I took advantage of it." But the bottom line to all this rationale is this: If you believe him, you have handed over the authority of this portion of your life to the great deceiver.

Let's return to the dark alleys analogy. Dark alleys contain three parts that mirror how we identify with our daily encounters with darkness: doorways, shadows, and dumpsters. Doorways are the choices we make whether to take part in sin or not; shadows come about when we allow the lies of darkness to violate light or truth; and dumpsters are where we throw away the evidence of our sins.

Doorways:

Every action we take is the product of a decision we make; it is a choice to do or not to do something based upon thought. "Should I click on that link?" "How can I cheat on my taxes in all of these grey areas?" "What do I do with that thought?" "Should I join him or her for drinks after work?" *Everything* we do, think, or say is a choice.

For followers of Jesus, it is a never-ending battle between spirit and flesh. What we know to be wrong in our heart is often the desire of the flesh. Whether it is lying, stealing, cheating, lust, or self-righteousness, these are the doorways we pass by all day long. Take one wrong doorway and the fallout can be devastating.

These doorways of life offer for the devil continuous opportunities to set up a stronghold in your life. To him, these temptations are a place where he can accuse you and punish you with shame and regret. He will do everything he can to set up shop in your life and he does so through two primary tools: fear and doubt.

Consider these questions as to how you've come face-to-face with Satan's schemes:

- What doorways have appeared to you that have peaked your curiosity enough to walk through?
- Which doorways that you've avoided so far have continued to show up?
- How do you feel emotionally when you walk through a door you know you shouldn't have?

> *No temptation has overtaken you except what is common to humanity.*
> *God is faithful and He will not allow you to be tempted beyond what you are able, but with temptation He will provide a way of escape, so that you are able to bear it. (1 Corinthians 10:13)*

Shadows:

Be aware that a disclaimer may be necessary for this section because of the amount of authority that has been yielded to the devil in the area of shadows. His divisive antics have led many to be offended. It has even become trendy to be offended because our opinions don't align in appropriate popular fashion. But keep in mind that offenses are not *given* to a person; they are *picked up and carried.* They cloud our vision and can trap whole segments of people—all in the name of political correctness or socially accepted norms. This is what Jesus had to say about it:

> *Woe to the world because of offenses. For offenses must come, but woe to that man by whom the offense comes. (Matthew 18:7)*

We are all a product of our environment. In fact, we learn from a young age to generally adapt to the character of the company we keep. In this regard, we're not unlike the chameleon who changes its appearance to blend in with its surroundings. Satan does the same thing; disguising himself to fit in wherever we are just to snag a foothold in order to influence us. It is his whole purpose—to cause division through lies and twisted truth in order to kill, steal, and destroy.

Shadows occur when the truth becomes warped, usually through the lenses of our worldview and the opinions that shape it. We all have opinions and perspectives gained from our life experiences. The key to remember in holding fast to our opinions is not whether they are right or wrong compared to others, but whether they are right or wrong when held against the truth of the Scriptures. Shadows occur in our lives when they don't align because they are, quite literally, the physical manifestation of darkness. Examine some of the shadows of your life and then ask yourself these questions:

- Which convictions do I have that cause the most division?
- In these convictions, what relationships have suffered the most through this division?
- Who influenced me in these convictions and out of what emotion?

And now hold your convictions up against these verses and this weighty quote. Ask yourself if your convictions are wholly truth-based.

> *There is a way that seems right to a man, but its end is the way to death. (Proverbs 14:12)*
> *The inexperienced believe anything, but the sensible watch their steps. (Proverbs 14:15)*
> *The eternal difference between right and wrong does not fluctuate, it is immutable. (Patrick Henry)*

Dumpsters:

The dumpsters of our lives are the most difficult areas to evaluate, accept, and confess. However, true healing can never happen until these dumpsters are opened safely, emptied, and their contents dealt with appropriately. That is because the dumpsters are where we hide the deepest of our hurts, our most secret sins, our mother and father wounds, and family dysfunctions. Oftentimes this is where fear, depression, and worthlessness take root in our souls. Perfectionism, striving, and comparison are usually birthed out of the hurts of our dumpsters. It is also the place where depravity holds us in bondage and doesn't allow us to live out our created purpose and it is where the enemy is at his most effective as a thief. That is because by hiding away our junk in our own private, closed away dumpster, we yield authority to him in these areas.

He starts by stripping us of our joy and holding it at bay, just outside our reach. When we transfer our joy to Satan he is free to manipulate or torture us at will. This is the same tactic he used with Adam and Eve when he convinced them to eat of the forbidden fruit. They acted on his promise of enlightenment and instantly realized the error of their way. They went from having true joy, all authority, peace, and freedom to suddenly having it all out of reach.

Below is what I consider to be the beginning steps toward a 'controlled opening' of your dumpster. Write your answers down and give them prayerful evaluation.

- When did I last experience overwhelming joy and peace?
- In what areas of my life do I feel shame?
- My anxiety spikes when I think about .
- What traumatic experiences have I gone through?

As you work through this process, work to commit these verses to memory.

> *He reveals the deep and hidden things; He knows what is in the darkness, and light dwells with Him. (Daniel 2:22)*
>
> *Don't participate in the fruitless works of darkness, but instead, expose them. For it is shameful even to mention what is done by them in secret. (Ephesians 5:11–12)*

Isn't it ironic that when we're hurt physically, we have no hesitation about going to the doctor, but when we are hurting spiritually and emotionally we think we can handle these aches on our own? Think about it this way: If we have something foreign in our body such as a cyst, or tumor, or thorn, we want it removed as soon as possible. That's because we understand the healing process can't begin until it is removed. It works just like this for our spiritual and emotional lives as well. Not only is our spiritual life tremendously important on its own, but Scripture tells us it breathes life into our physical health as well. It's worth noting that the impact can be positive or negative.

> *A joyful heart is good medicine, but a broken spirit dries up the bones. (Proverbs 17:22)*
>
> *Dear friend, I pray that you may prosper in every way and be in good health, just as your soul prospers. (3 John 1:2)*
>
> *But have nothing to do with irreverent and silly myths. Rather, train yourself in godliness, for, the training of the body has a limited benefit, but godliness is beneficial in every way, since it holds promise for the present life and also for the life to come. (1 Timothy 4:7–8)*

Don't consider yourself to be wise; fear the LORD and turn away from evil. This will be healing for your body and strengthening for your bones. (Proverbs 3:7–8)

For most of us, our dumpster contents have haunted us for years. We carry unnecessary hurt, shame, and disgust that ultimately leads us to live a life centered on fear of being found out. The thought of judgment and pointing fingers can be absolutely paralyzing and that is exactly where the prince of darkness wants you. One of the most damaging lies we believe is that we will be met with judgment instead of love. No matter what you have experienced before, the life of Jesus established unshakeable truth that should bring comfort to all His followers.

Everything exposed by the light is made clear, for what makes everything clear is light. (Ephesians 5:13–14)

For judgment is without mercy to the one who hasn't shown mercy. Mercy triumphs over judgment. (James 2:13)

Above all, keep your love for one another at full strength, since love covers a multitude of sins. (1 Peter 4:8)

Indeed, we have all received grace after grace from His fullness, for although the law was given through Moses, grace and truth came through Jesus Christ. (John 1:16–17)

Answering the questions presented earlier in the chapter is the first step toward evaluating the contents of your dumpster. It's a major step forward just to agree to open it. For me personally, this was he most difficult step, closely followed by the battle of preparing for confession.

The night before I committed to opening my personal dumpster, I could hear the devil speak lie after lie to me. Having the knowledge of Ephesians 6:12 firmly planted in my heart, I was able to identify his spiteful lies and rely upon the Holy Spirit to remind me of verse after verse of Scripture to shine the light of truth upon his darkness. It was truly a faith deepening experience to behold as I was granted vision of the battle before me. To envision the fiery darts of the enemy extinguished as proclaimed in Ephesians 6:16 was an awesome and humbling experience.

> *In every situation take the shield of faith, And with it you will be able to extinguish All the flaming arrows of the evil one. (Ephesians 6:16)*
>
> *Therefore, confess your sins to one another and pray for one another, so that you may be healed. The intense prayer of the righteous is very powerful. (James 5:16)*
>
> *If we confess our sins, He is faithful and righteous to forgive us our sins and to cleanse us from all unrighteousness. (1 John 1:9)*

As you work toward bringing the contents of your dumpster to light, know that you are not alone in this process. There are three tools that will help you immeasurably as you make your walkthrough confession: a Bible, prayer, and wise counsel. The power in each of these cannot be overstated. Each, in their own way, will serve you well to seek out.

> *Lord, You are my lamp; The Lord illuminates my darkness. (2 Samuel 22:29)*
>
> *Your word is a lamp for my feet, and a light on my path. (Psalm 119:105)*

I have found there is truth in the old adage that claims the Bible has the answers to everything. The more I study it, the clearer it becomes. Sure, we're lots more technically advanced than back in Jesus's day, but so very many of our issues and concerns and problems are strikingly similar. Our clothes, and homes, and methods of transportation may be different, but we're not so far removed. These verses apply now just as much as they did then.

I often search the Internet for Scripture whenever I need clarity about something. In less than a few seconds I can have every relevant verse as it pertains to my struggle or subject. Without fail, every time I work my way through these verses the answer becomes clear. Not a day goes by for me without searching Scripture for an answer. There are also some great Bible apps for your smartphone or tablet with search features and topical teachings. I personally use the YouVersion® Bible app for word searches. It also has a 'verse of the day,' highlighting and sharing options, and is free.

For believers, prayer is our 24/7 direct line to Christ. To be able to communicate with the Creator of the universe is an unbelievably awesome privilege. The verses that follow show how Jesus taught the disciples to pray as He did. Praying, individually or with a prayer partner, is a great way to gain clarity. It is also helpful to participate in intercessory prayer, meaning allowing others to pray on your behalf and you praying for them. Because God is relational, He will always hear your appeal, honor your worship, and be constant in His character. James, Jesus's half-brother, put it like this:

> *Now if any of you lacks wisdom, he should ask God, who gives to all generously and without criticizing, and it will be given to him.*
>
> *But let him ask in faith without doubting. For the doubter is like the surging sea, driven and tossed by the wind. (James 1:5–6)*
>
> *Is anyone among you suffering? He should pray. Is anyone cheerful? He should sing praises. (James 5:13)*

Therefore, you should pray like this; Our Father in heaven, Your name be honored as holy.

Your kingdom come, Your will be done, on earth as it is in heaven. Give us today our daily bread, And forgive us our debts, as we also have forgiven our debtors.

And do not bring us into temptation, but deliver us from the evil one. For Yours is the kingdom and the power and the glory forever. Amen. (Matthew 6:9–13)

Wise counsel is yet another way to gain understanding and instruction during times of confusion. Please understand that wisdom and knowledge are different. Knowledge is information-based; wisdom is the appropriate use of knowledge. Solomon is considered the wisest man who ever lived and much of his wisdom can be found in the book of Proverbs. It is a great place to find wisdom to be used in our daily lives to steer clear of Satan's continuous traps. Remember, he sees every day as a new opportunity to steal, kill, and destroy all of us.

All the ways of a man seem right to him, but the LORD evaluates the motives. (Proverbs 21:2)

Listen to instruction and be wise; don't ignore it. (Proverbs 8:33)

For followers of Jesus, this is where it is important to have the Holy Spirit as your best friend. If you have read this far and are not yet a follower of Jesus, my hope is that this book has played a part in His pursuit of relationship with you and you for Him. It is the ultimate honor to be considered a vessel used for His glory. If you are tired of striving, running, chasing something, and always feeling empty, there is hope and freedom available to you in the mighty name of Jesus, the Light. I pray you can hear Him calling you today.

Come to Me, all of you who are weary and burdened, and I will give you rest.

All of you, take up My yoke and learn from Me, because I am gentle and humble in heart, and you will find rest for yourselves.

For My yoke is easy and My burden is light. (Matthew 11:28–30)

For you are called to freedom, brothers; only don't use this freedom as an opportunity for the flesh, but serve one another through love. (Galatians 5:13)

Christ has liberated us to be free. Stand firm then and don't submit again to a yoke of slavery. (Galatians 5:1)

CHAPTER 4

DEPRAVITY IS OUR CHOICE—HOPE EXISTS

Jesus told him, "I am the way, the truth, and the life.
No one comes to the Father except through Me." (John 14:6)

The life of the Apostle Paul is an amazing story of transformation and restoration. He went from killing Christians to preaching the message of Jesus in just three days. He authored almost a third of the New Testament through his letters of encouragement, correction, and instruction. In his letters, he called people to a life of righteousness according to the grace, mercy, and forgiveness of Jesus that had transformed his life. As we evaluate this most awesome account, reflect on the following verse:

Jesus said, "I come into this world for judgment, in order that those who do not see will see and those who do see will become blind." (John 9:39)

Saul of Tarsus was born somewhere around 5 AD. As a boy, he was educated by Gamaliel in the law of Moses and the prophets according to the strict view of patriarchal law. As a Pharisee and teacher of the law, Gamaliel was respected by all the people. In these days (and even now), the religious were strict followers of the law and hated the message of grace Jesus had come to teach. Their hatred was passed to Saul as he watched and approved of the stoning of the first Christian martyr, Stephen. As the witnesses laid their robes at his feet, Saul took on the title of Persecutor. Saul was a leader in this hatred of those who followed Jesus and His teachings because they were not logical according to the law. In fact, he sought many out, dragging them out of their houses and putting them in prison.

Meanwhile, Saul was still breathing threats and murder against the disciples of the Lord. He went to the high priest and requested letters from him to the synagogues in Damascus, so that if he found any men or women who belonged to the Way, he might bring them as prisoners to Jerusalem.

As he traveled and was nearing Damascus, a light from heaven suddenly flashed around him. Falling to the ground, he heard a voice saying to him, "Saul, Saul, why are you persecuting Me?" "Who are You, Lord?" he said.

"I am Jesus, the One you are persecuting," He replied. "But get up and go into the city, and you will be told what you must do."

The men who were traveling with him stood speechless, hearing the sound but seeing no one. Then Saul got up from the ground, and though his eyes were open, he could see nothing. So they took him by the hand and led him

*into Damascus. He was unable to see for three days and
did not eat or drink.*

*There was a disciple in Damascus named Ananias.
And the Lord said to him in a vision, "Ananias!" "Here I
am, Lord!"*

*He said. "Get up and go to the street called Straight,"
the Lord said to him, "to the house of Judas, and ask for
a man from Tarsus named Saul, since he is praying there.
In a vision he has seen a man named Ananias coming in
and placing his hands on him so he can regain his sight."*

*"Lord," Ananias answered, "I have heard from many
people about this man, how much harm he has done to
Your saints in Jerusalem. And he has authority here from
the chief priests to arrest all who call on Your name."*

*But the Lord said to him, "Go! For this man is My
chosen instrument to take My name to the Gentiles, kings,
and the Israelites. I will show him how much he must suffer
for My name!" So Ananias left and entered the house.*

*Then he placed his hands on him and said, "Brother
Saul, the Lord Jesus, who appeared to you on the road you
were traveling, has sent me so that you can regain your sight
and be filled with the Holy Spirit." At once something like
scales fell from his eyes, and he regained his sight. Then he
got up and was baptized. And after taking some food, he
regained his strength. (Acts 9:1–19)*

While I could have paraphrased the happenings in Acts 9, I believe
it is more effective taken directly from Scripture. Saul, who was also
known as Paul, preached the gospel of Jesus Christ from the day of his
transformation forward. I guess you could say that 'he saw the light' on
the Damascus road, and over those three days of blindness, the truth
was illuminated. In an instant, we see the speed of light (suddenly)
penetrating the darkness (Saul's heart). We can see the calling and
transformation of Saul, God's chosen instrument, who was to carry the
banner of Christ to all people.

Because of this charge, Paul spent a good amount of time after his conversion in prison. It was during this time that he penned most of the letters in the New Testament. Paul, even though bold in his proclamation of Christ, remained a humble man throughout his ministry. Even in his letters, he deflected any elevation of himself. He understood his power came through the Holy Spirit and his authority was found in the name of Jesus and that he was but a messenger.

All scripture is inspired by God and is profitable for teaching, for rebuking, for correcting, for training in righteousness, so that the man of God may be complete, equipped for every good work. (2 Timothy 3:16–17)

Paul's mission was clear: to share the gospel of Jesus to all who would listen. He understood the legalistic measure of the law required grace. So, when he was transformed on the road to Damascus, he wanted to share the grace extended to him by Jesus, the new covenant. Prior to that experience, he had heard the story of Jesus and all that He did, even to death on the cross, but still considered himself righteously driven to stop what he called The Way.

One of the biggest misunderstandings the Pharisees and others who followed the Levitical Law held was the requirement of sacrifice for the atonement of sin. They were so accustomed to the requirements of the law, they ignored the fulfillment of prophetic scripture.

> *Don't assume that I came to destroy the Law of the Prophets. I did not come to destroy but to fulfill. (Matthew 5:17)*

These are the words of Jesus as part of His greatest sermon ever, the Sermon on the Mount. In fulfilling the law, he was often referred to as the Messiah or Immanuel, meaning God is with us. Jesus also spoke of Himself as the atoning sacrifice for all sin (1 John 2:2) and as the Spotless Lamb (1 Peter 1:19) that was required by the law. He knew His purpose for coming to earth was to dwell among us.

> *For God loved the world in this way: He gave His One and Only Son, so that everyone who believes in Him will not perish but have eternal life.*
>
> *For God did not send His Son into the world that He might condemn the world, but that the world might be saved through Him. Anyone who believes in Him is not condemned, but anyone who does not believe is already condemned, because he has not believed in the name of the One and Only Son of God.*
>
> *This, then, is the judgment: the light has come into the world, and people loved darkness rather than the light because their deeds were evil. For everyone who practices wicked things hates the light and avoids it, so that his deeds may not be exposed. But anyone who lives by the truth comes to the light, so that his works may be shown to be accomplished by God. (John 3:16–21)*

One of the letters Paul wrote was to the people of Rome. Because Paul inherited Roman citizenship, he wanted to carry the good news of Jesus to his fellow citizens and to let them know he was coming to them. Because the message of Jesus was threatening to Roman leaders, Paul was quickly placed in prison. Like many of us when our control is threatened, the Roman rulers of the time were uncomfortable with Paul's teachings. Darkness caused them to reject his words.

During this time in prison, Paul wrote his last letter to Timothy. In it, he encouraged Timothy to fulfill his ministry and gave him important instructions and updates. He also let Timothy know that his time was drawing near. Soon after, Paul was martyred. He was beheaded because his legal status as a Roman citizen protected him from crucifixion.

I would be remiss if I didn't share what is called the Roman Road. These seven verses are a collection that offer a clear and structured path to acceptance of Jesus Christ as savior and king. *Your Savior and King.*

You may be a great person intent on trying to do great things, but your actions or deeds cannot and will not *ever* earn you access to the Heavenly Father. On the flip side, you might be thinking that the things you have done are unforgivable and that you could never be allowed into heaven. If that were the case, it would effectively mean Jesus's blood, shed on the cross, was not enough to cover your sins and that is simply *not* the case. This unfounded belief not only speaks against the law of the prophets, but is also a lie from the pit of hell. There is nothing the devil would like more than for any would-be Christ-followers to believe that. That said, in honor of the life of Paul and for the glory of Jesus Christ, *the* Savior, I light this path to Jesus by sharing these scriptures with you:

The Roman Road:

1. We must resolve that God is the Creator of everything and accept our humble position in God's purpose.

From the creation of the world His invisible attributes, that is, His eternal power and divine nature, have been clearly seen, being understood by what He has made. As a result, people are without excuse. For though they knew God, they did not glorify Him as God or show gratitude. Instead, their thinking became nonsense, and their senseless minds were darkened. (Romans 1:20–21)

2. We must realize our imperfection and sinful nature as people. None of us are worthy under God's standards.

   For all have sinned and fall short of the glory of God. (Romans 3:23)

3. God showed His mercy by giving us a way to have our sins forgiven. He showed His love by giving us the possibility to have life through the death of His Son, Jesus Christ.

   For while we were still helpless, at the appointed moment, Christ died for the ungodly. For rarely will someone die for a just person—though for a good person perhaps someone might even dare to die. But God proves His own love for us in that while we were still sinners Christ died for us! (Romans 5:6–8)

4. If we remain in our sin, we are destined to die. However, if we receive Jesus as our Lord and Savior, and repent of our sins, we will have eternal life.

   For the wages of sin is death, but the gift of God is eternal life in Jesus Christ our Lord. (Romans 6:23)

5. You will be saved when you confess that Jesus is Lord and believe in your heart that God raised Him from the dead.

   If you confess with your mouth, "Jesus is Lord," and believe in your heart that God raised Him from the dead, you will be saved. With the heart one believes, resulting in righteousness, and with the mouth one confesses, resulting in salvation. (Romans 10:9–10)

6.   This is not about religion or rituals, but relationship. Remember He desires relationship.

> *For everyone who calls on the name of the Lord will be saved. (Romans 10:13)*

7.   He is worthy, and ready to be Lord of your life today.

> *For from Him and through Him and to Him are all things. To Him be the glory forever. Amen. (Romans 11:36)*

My prayer is that if you are not a follower of Jesus and are ready to accept God's free gift of salvation that you will take the path of the Roman Road set before you. This is a prayerful guideline for your heartfelt step of faith:

"Father God, I know that I have broken your laws and my sins have separated me from You. I am truly sorry and now desire to follow You and turn from my past life. Please forgive me, and help me to keep from sinning. Thank You for Your Son, Jesus, who died for my sins, defeated death on the cross, is alive, and hears my prayers today. Jesus, I surrender my life to You, to rule and reign in my heart from this day forward. Be the Lord of my life today. Send Your Holy Spirit to guide me in my daily walk and change me from the inside to do Your will. In the mighty name of Jesus, I pray. Amen."

> *"Repent," Peter said to them, "and be baptized, each of you, in the name of Jesus the Messiah for the forgiveness of your sins, and you will receive the gift of the Holy Spirit." (Acts 2:38)*
>
> *As many as I love, I rebuke and discipline. So be committed and repent. Listen! I stand at the door and knock. If anyone hears My voice and opens the door, I will come in to him and have dinner with him, and he with Me. The victor: I will give him the right to sit with Me on*

*My throne, just as I won the victory and sat down with My
Father on His throne. (Revelation 3:19–21)*

If you decided to receive Jesus today, you are now considered a
son or daughter of the King. Like any new relationship, it needs to be
nurtured and invested in. If you are here, I can assure you Jesus has
been pursuing you and is rejoicing that you've answered the call. Here
are some ways to grow in your new commitment to Jesus:

- Find a spirit-led, Bible-believing church where you can
  worship God;
- Tell someone else about your new faith in Christ;
- Get baptized; this is your first step of obedience according
  to Scripture;
- Spend time with God each day; develop a habit of reading the
  Bible and spending time in prayer. Ask God to increase your
  faith and your understanding of His word; find a Bible-reading
  plan to guide you;
- Find fellowship with other followers of Jesus; it is important to
  have a group to support you andw to turn to with questions.

Remember that we take on the character of our environment, so
you need to evaluate the company you are keeping. Ask the Holy Spirit
to help you identify areas of toxicity in your life. He will be faithful to
let you know, but it will be your choice to change.

*Do not be deceived: "Bad company corrupts good
morals." (1 Corinthians 15:33)*

If you have now accepted Jesus, you have made the most impactful
decision of your life. As a fellow believer, I am extremely proud of you
and excited for your future. If you fully embrace and engage in your
relationship with Him, your life will never be the same. It won't always
be easy, but it will be different and infinitely better in the long run.
Rejoice new believer! Your name is now written in the Book of Life! You
will spend all of eternity in heaven with God. And you have for your
remaining days on earth the Holy Spirit as your personal guide. Your
sins are forgiven, and you are seen by Him as righteous!

CHAPTER 5

AUTHORITY & WHY SATAN HATES LIGHT

Let no one deceive you with empty arguments, for because of these things God's wrath is coming on the disobedient. Therefore, do not become their partners. For you were once darkness, but now you are light in the Lord. Walk as children of light—for the fruit of light results in all goodness, righteousness, and truth—discerning what is pleasing to the Lord. (Ephesians 5:6–10)

Most of us remember a time in our childhood when we enjoyed a special privilege as long as we followed the rules and obeyed. But once we became disobedient or abused the privilege, it was taken away. Remember the emotions and the sadness from that time of loss? It was heartbreaking in the moment. Fast forward a few decades. We're older, presumably wiser, and probably carrying loads more responsibility in lots of different areas. Now consider the fallout from neglect or abuse of these elevated responsibilities: it is remarkably more far-reaching and deeply consequential and that's as it should be. Because of this, there exists in our lack of understanding, a place where the consequences of our actions seem to overshadow any grace that has been extended, and rightfully so. Even Jesus addressed this relationship between privilege and responsibility:

And that slave who knew his master's will and didn't prepare himself or do it will be severely beaten.

> *But the one who did not know and did things deserving*
> *of blows will be beaten lightly. Much will be required of*
> *everyone who has been given much.*
> *And even more will be expected of the one who has been*
> *entrusted with more. (Luke 12:47–48)*

With this in mind, allow me to trace Satan's early days and all that he was originally entrusted with. Contrary to what so many of us have believed at one time, he wasn't created as a mean-spirited little guy with horns and a pitchfork.

> *He is the image of the invisible God, the firstborn*
> *over all creation; because by Him everything was created,*
> *in heaven and on earth, the visible and the invisible,*
> *whether thrones or dominions or rulers or authorities—*
> *all things have been created through Him and for Him.*
> *(Colossians 1:15–16)*
> *All things were created through Him, and apart from*
> *Him not one thing was created that has been created.*
> *(John 1:3)*

In both of these Scriptures, Jesus is the reference and the confirmation of His existence from the beginning as the second part of the Trinity; Father, Son, and Holy Spirit. Everything that has ever been created was created by Him—even the heavens. And Satan.

> *For everything created by God is good, and nothing*
> *should be rejected if it is received with thanksgiving,*
> *since it is sanctified by the word of God and by prayer. (1*
> *Timothy 4:4)*

Originally known as Lucifer, Satan hasn't always been the standard against which all evil is measured. In fact, the name Lucifer is translated from the Hebrew word 'helel' meaning 'brightness.' The designation of the name Lucifer is as the representation of the 'morning star.' In order to get a better picture of how Lucifer, or Satan, was created and his original purpose, we have to pay close attention to the words of the prophets.

The best information comes from the following lament (or grief expression) which was given to Ezekiel by the Lord to address Satan as a powerful influencer of the King of Tyre:

> *You were the seal of perfection, full of wisdom and perfect in beauty. You were in Eden, the garden of God. Every kind of precious stone covered you: carnelian, topaz, and diamond, beryl, onyx, and jasper, sapphire, turquoise and emerald. Your mountings and settings were created in gold; they were prepared on the day you were created. You were an anointed guardian cherub, for I had appointed you. You were on the holy mountain of God; you walked among the fiery stones. From the day you were created you were blameless in your ways until wickedness was found in you. Through the abundance of your trade, you were filled with violence, and you sinned. So I expelled you in disgrace from the mountain of God, and banished you, guardian cherub, from among the fiery stones. Your heart became proud because of your beauty; For the sake of your splendor you corrupted your wisdom. So I threw you down to the earth. (Ezekiel 28:12b–17a)*

Lucifer was created spectacularly beautiful and placed in a high, if not the highest, angelic position. Being appointed as guardian cherub on the holy mountain of God was undoubtedly an honorable and weighty appointment. For God to lament, He must have cared deeply for him and deeply grieved his fall from his heavenly appointment. Much authority was given to Lucifer, and when humility failed him and pride consumed him, he was cast down to earth.

Here is the second time God addressed Satan through a message, this time to the King of Babylon by the prophet Isaiah:

> *Shining morning star, how you have fallen from the heavens! You destroyer of nations, you have been cut down*

to the ground. You said to yourself: "I will ascend to the heavens; I will set up my throne above the stars of God. I will sit on the mount of the god's assembly, in the remotest parts of the North. I will ascend above the highest clouds; I will make myself like the Most High." But you will be brought down to Sheol into the deepest regions of the Pit. (Isaiah 14:12–15)

God spoke to Lucifer and immediately put a stop to his plans. In modern day talk, he told Lucifer, "About your plans not going to happen. And besides that, you're going to hell. With your angels. Forever."

So the great dragon was thrown out—the ancient serpent, who is called the devil and Satan, the one who deceives the whole world. He was thrown to earth, and his angels with him. (Revelation 12:9)

Now that we have a better idea of who Satan is, why he fell, and why he harbors so much hatred for those who reflect the light of Christ, we can begin to better understand authority and where it comes from.

Everyone must submit to the governing authorities, for there is no authority except from God, and those that exist are instituted by God. So then, the one who resists the authority is opposing God's command, and those who oppose it will bring judgment on themselves. (Romans 13:1–2)

It is important to understand that the One who created the heavens and the earth has ALL authority. Those who are given authority by Him are subject to His authority. In other words, they are dependent on His appointment *for their authority*. This is where trust and faith are required for followers of Jesus. Many times, we see people given authority that in NO WAY makes sense to us, but we must always be mindful that God is not in any way surprised or confined to our understanding of any situation. It is in these times that we are to take to heart the Lord's declaration through the prophet Isaiah:

For as heaven is higher than earth, My ways are higher than your ways, and My thoughts than your thoughts.

For just as rain and snow fall from heaven, and do not return there without saturating the earth, and making it germinate and sprout, and providing seed to sow and food to eat, so My word that comes from My mouth will not return to me empty, but it will accomplish what I please, and will prosper in what I send it to do. (Isaiah 55:9–11)

And His admonition in Proverbs:

Trust in the LORD with all your heart, and do not rely on your own understanding; think about Him in all your ways, and He will guide you on the right paths. (Proverbs 3:5–6)

Throughout Scripture it is evident that authority is given, not taken. Any authority given is subject to the giver. It is imperative to understand this as a believer, but even more so for those who are not yet true followers of Jesus.

The first authority given on earth was to Adam as God appointed him to 'watch' over the garden of Eden and rule over the creatures of the earth. Adam, while being made in the image of God, still had free will in his flesh. This free will is God-ordained because as much as He desires relationship with all creation, He will never force Himself on us. Since Adam and Eve had free will, they were able to make their own choices when Satan showed up as the serpent. And that's when things went a little haywire:

Now the serpent was the most cunning of all the wild animals that the LORD God had made. He said to the woman, "Did God really say, 'You can't eat from any tree in the garden'?" The woman said to the serpent, "We may eat the fruit from the trees in the garden. But about the fruit of the tree in the middle of the garden, God said, 'You must not eat it or touch it, or you will die.'"

"No! You will not die," the serpent said to the woman. "In fact, God knows that when you eat it your eyes will be opened and you will be like God, knowing good and evil."

Then the woman saw that the tree was good for food and delightful to look at, and that it was desirable for obtaining wisdom. So she took some of its fruit and ate it; she also gave some to her husband, who was with her, and he ate it.

Then the eyes of both of them were opened, and they knew they were naked; so they sewed fig leaves and made loincloths for themselves. (Genesis 3:1–7)

Scripture is clear that Satan was adorned in beauty, so it was rather easy to attract the attention of Eve. Once he had her attention, Satan called into question the instruction God had given them regarding the Tree of the Knowledge of Good and Evil—the *only* boundary for them in the garden. Just by planting a seed of doubt, Satan deceived them into compromising their trust of God and His words, but still, they made the decision to act on their own. He didn't force the fruit upon them; he simply wooed them into a spirit of rebellion. The fruit was the same as all of the other trees except that it was forbidden *by God*. This simple story provides such a powerful testimony of the weaknesses found in our humanity: we always want the things that we can't or don't have.

The tenth commandment, "Do not covet," is there for a reason. When we focus on the things we don't have, we fail to see the things we do. This is what happened in the garden when Adam yielded his authority to Satan. The result? Adam and Eve ate the fruit, felt the shame, and then tried to hide from God—one sin begetting another and then another.

We have established through Scripture that all authority comes from God, the Father. It follows, then, that Jesus, being fully man (flesh) and fully God (Spirit), was also given all authority from the Father:

Jesus spoke these things, looked up to heaven, and said: Father, the hour has come. Glorify Your Son so that the Son may glorify You, for You gave Him authority over all flesh; so He may give eternal life to all You have given Him. This is eternal life: that they may know You, the only true God, and the One You have sent—Jesus Christ. (John 17:1–3)

Then Jesus came near and said to them, "All authority has been given to Me in heaven and on earth. Go, therefore, and make disciples of all nations, baptizing them in the name of the Father and of the Son and of the Holy Spirit, teaching them to observe everything I have commanded you. And remember, I am with you always, to the end of the age." (Matthew 28:18–20)

Jesus knew that taking on flesh made Him vulnerable to all of the temptation and sin that we face. Because of that, He lowered Himself to be subject to the Father and obedient to His calling and purpose here on earth; to live a sinless life and be the spotless lamb, sacrificed for the sins of the world to those who receive His grace and come into relationship with Him as Savior and King. Knowing this, Satan was quick to tempt Jesus in His weakest moments throughout His time on earth. The motives and tactics of Satan can be clearly seen in the first temptation of Jesus:

Then Jesus returned from the Jordan, full of the Holy Spirit, and was led by the Spirit in the wilderness for forty days to be tempted by the devil. He ate nothing during those days and when they were over, He was hungry. The devil said to Him, "If You are the Son of God, tell this stone to become bread."

But Jesus answered him, "It is written: Man must not live on bread alone."

So he took Him up and showed Him all the kingdoms of the world in a moment of time. The devil said to Him, "I will give You their splendor and all this authority, because it has been given over to me, and I can give it to anyone I want. If You, then, will worship me, all will be Yours."

And Jesus answered him, "It is written:

Worship the Lord your God, and serve Him only."

So he took Him to Jerusalem, had Him stand on the pinnacle of the temple, and said to Him, "If You are the Son of God, throw Yourself down from here. For it is written: He will give His angels orders concerning you, and they will support you with their hands, so that you will not strike your foot against a stone.

And Jesus answered him, "It is said: Do not test the Lord your God."

After the devil had finished every temptation, he departed from Him for a time. (Luke 4:1–13)

It is evident that Satan knows Scripture and can and will use it to deceive us. It is also proof that he is a liar and is on a mission to gain the authority that was never given to him. Scripture in the hands of evil can be a dangerous weapon and Satan is no exception. He can twist it and use it out of context to manipulate people. He can empower false teachers and use the holy for unholy purposes. He stopped at nothing to try and elevate himself against Jesus and he will stop at nothing in dealing with us either. He knew Jesus had been given all authority and would yield it all to him if He worshipped him, but Jesus rebuked him using Scripture. The best—*the only*— way not to fall victim to misinterpretation and misrepresentation is following Jesus's example by knowing Scripture and being in relationship with the Holy Spirit.

There is only one instance in the Bible where Satan is given authority—the Book of Job. Actually, it was more like he was given permission rather than authority and that's because it served God's purpose to illuminate a blind spot Job had. In the end, however, God was glorified and Job's possessions were restored twice over leaving him more blessed than before his trials.

Jesus calls Satan the "ruler of this world" in several verses (John 12:31, John 14:30, and John 16:11) but what is the breadth and depth of Jesus' authority? These verses provide some insight:

> *The seventy returned with joy saying, "Lord, even the demons submit to us in Your name." He said to them, "I watched Satan fall from heaven like a lightening flash. Look, I have given you the authority to trample on snakes and scorpions and over all the power of the enemy; nothing will even harm you. However, don't rejoice that the spirits submit to you, but rejoice that your names are written in heaven." (Luke 10:17–20)*
>
> *I assure you: The one who believes in Me will also do the works that I do. And he will do even greater works than these, because I am going to the Father. Whatever you ask in My name, I will do it so that the Father may be glorified in the Son. If you ask Me anything in My name, I will do it. (John 14:12–14)*
>
> *Before this faith came, we were confined under the law, imprisoned until the coming faith was revealed. The law, then, was our guardian until Christ, so that we could be justified by faith. But since that faith has come, we are no longer under a guardian, for you are all sons of God through faith in Christ Jesus. (Galatians 3:23–26)*
>
> *For His divine power has given us everything required for life and godliness, through the knowledge of Him who called us by His own glory and goodness.*
>
> *By these He has given us very great and precious promises, so that through them you may share in the divine nature, escaping the corruption that is in the world because of evil desires.*
>
> *For this very reason, make every effort to supplement your faith with goodness, goodness with knowledge, knowledge with self-control, self-control with endurance,*

endurance with godliness, godliness with brotherly affection, and brotherly affection with love.

For if these qualities are yours and are increasing, they will keep you from being useless or unfruitful in the knowledge of our Lord Jesus Christ. (2 Peter 1:3–8)

These are just a few verses that establish how God sees us as true followers of Jesus and the power and authority that is given to us as heirs of Jesus, earned by His blood shed on the cross. As sacred heirs, we have been given everything Jesus was given, including authority. But where does Satan get his authority to rule in and over our lives? Remember the grey areas of our lives—those dark alleyways where we hide our junk and where we have allowed truth to be warped into a compromised world view? And those doorways we are tempted to walk through but know we shouldn't? These are the areas where we yield authority to Satan. He is slow, calculated, and ready to pounce on what is not his, taking without asking, when the opportunity presents itself. But worry not, friend. Through confession and repentance and a growing relationship with Christ, we can reclaim that lost ground. When we heed the power of God's Word, darkness has no power over *His light in our lives.*

The night is nearly over, and the daylight is near, so let us discard the deeds of darkness and put on the armor of light. (Romans 13:12)

But you are a chosen race, a royal priesthood, a holy nation, a people for His possession, so that you may proclaim the praises of the One who called you out of darkness into His marvelous light. (1 Peter 2:9)

It is our decision how much power and authority we yield to the enemy. He is here to steal it from you and will take advantage of every opportunity you offer him. As believers, our power is directly correlated to our surrender to the Father, time spent in Scripture and prayer, and the strength of our relationship with Holy Spirit. Without

Jesus, we are all defenseless to the devil's scheme and tactics. There is no other defense.

> *Finally, be strengthened by the Lord and by* His vast strength. Put on the full armor of God so that you can stand against the tactics of the Devil. (Ephesians 6:10–11)

CHAPTER 6

THE FALLACY OF GREY AREAS

It is my prayer that by reading this book you now see how we have all, at one time or another, bought into a deception that warped the truth and caused us to trust our own fallible understanding. I would be lying to you if I told you that it never happens to me. I can promise it happens to us all. We are all easy targets for the enemy, especially when we elevate ourselves and act out of a posture of pride, accomplishments, or knowledge. Please know that it is from a position of humility that I have written this book and for no glory of my own. If this weren't my sole motivation, I would be even more vulnerable to further and stronger enemy influence. We all need to continually evaluate our stances and beliefs.

For the longest time I bought into the 'grey area' verbiage, only to find out I was being deceived and robbed of so much true peace, joy, and freedom, which was established through Christ Jesus when He fulfilled the law of the prophets. The spiritual influence of my dumpster contents bled over into the shadows of my life leaving me with a warped truth that was guised under a veil of protection and self-justification.

We must choose whom we are going to follow. Eternity began a long time ago and will go on forever. Heaven and hell most certainly exist; there is no middle ground. All of us will eventually end up in one or the other after we die, but the time to decide is *now*. The failure to choose one or the other IS a choice unto itself. We can see this truth in Revelation in the letter to the church of Laodicea:

I know your works, that you are neither cold or hot. So, because you are lukewarm, and neither hot nor cold, I am going to vomit you out of My mouth.

Because you say, 'I'm rich; I have become wealthy, and need nothing,' and you don't know that you are wretched, pitiful, poor, blind, and naked, I advise you to buy from Me gold refined in the fire so that you may be rich, and white clothes so that you may be dressed and your shameful nakedness not be exposed, and ointment to spread on your eyes so that you may see.

As many as I love, I rebuke and discipline. So be committed and repent. (Revelation 3:15–19)

Here we see that there is no middle ground; no fence walkers. God is calling us all to take a stand on one side or the other; to commit or quit. This is the same call Jesus gave in the Sermon on the Mount:

But I tell you, don't take an oath at all: either by heaven, because it is God's throne; or by the earth, because it is His footstool; or by Jerusalem, because it is the city of the Great King. Neither should you swear by your head, because you cannot make a single hair white or black. But let your word 'yes' be 'yes,' and your 'no' be 'no.' Anything more than this is from the evil one. (Matthew 5:34–37)

Jesus is unwavering when He speaks of the 'grey areas' we all face. He tells us straightforward—they are from the devil because when we operate in the middle ground, we are effectively choosing him over Christ. That's his territory, his area of greatest influence, his sweet spot of opportunity to keep us from strengthening our resolve to live for Christ. We may think we're living in the in-between spot, choosing neither Christ nor Satan, but we're not. When we choose not to live for Christ, we are, by default, giving Satan authority over our lives. It may seem unthreatening at first, but beware—it is darkness that has been created by warped or watered-down truth.

Satan is the ultimate deceiver and wants us all to believe that half-truths are good enough and still make us good people. But hear this again: *there is no middle ground, no minor or insignificant half-truths.* There are only truths and lies. Satan knows this; he just doesn't want us to know this.

As I write this, I think about our society and how divided we are. Many of the opinions we are acting on have no foundational basis; they're simply our opinions. They are not backed by any provisions or promises but are oftentimes defended as if they were undis- putable truths. When we become so enamored with what we think is right (whether it truly is or not), we close the door to understanding or accepting any civil or responsible corrective measures or dialogue that might bring clarity, peace, and understanding.

It's not unlike a two-year-old throwing a fit because, at the center of our irrational actions, we have forgotten the key commandment— to love one another. By the time this happens, we have become a pawn to be played by the evil one and have given him permission to use us as he wishes. And don't even begin to believe you've got all the guilt and shame your dumpster can hold; Satan would love to fill another one just as brimming over. In the end we have to choose who we will serve throughout our lifetimes. When we keep in mind that there is a bigger picture that awaits us all, it makes the choice considerably easier.

> *He (God) made the One (Jesus) who did not know sin to be sin for us, so that we might become the righteousness of God in Him. (2 Corinthians 5:21)*

Because we were created in the image of God, He has called us to righteousness through the life, death, and resurrection of Jesus Christ. There was no darkness in Jesus, so if we want to be on the side of light, it is up to us to set Christ as the example. This means constantly working to emulate His mind, His speech, His actions, and His heart. None of these challenges are simple and without testing. But Jesus taught us how to live, exemplifying in every action the Fruit of the Spirit—love, joy, peace, patience, kindness, goodness, faithfulness, gentleness, and self-control. Master these and your life will honor Christ.

Keep in mind that every action is the result of a decision— conscious or otherwise. Jesus measured every action against these attributes. Those who follow Him are called righteous through the power of His blood shed for the sins of the world; those who don't, sadly are not. Jesus died for you. And me. And everyone who would come after Him and call Him by name. The way Jesus lived *and died* is proof that righteousness is not found in being right, but rather through a relationship with God and putting Him first in your life.

> *Therefore, fear the LORD and worship Him in sincerity and truth. Get rid of all the gods your ancestors worshipped beyond the Euphrates River and in Egypt, and worship the LORD. But if it doesn't please you to worship the LORD, choose for yourselves today the one you will worship: the gods your fathers worshipped beyond the Euphrates River, or the gods of the Amorites in whose land you are living. As for me and my family, we will worship the LORD. (Joshua 24:14–15)*

Joshua was calling the Israelites to make a choice. God had delivered them from bondage in Egypt and led them to the promised land under His protective watch. But the Israelites did not come without baggage— literally. They brought with them the man-made idols of their ancestors despite the provisions of the Lord. But Joshua knew the Lord would not share His throne of worship and told the Israelites they must rid themselves of the foreign gods and offer their hearts to Him. When they agreed, a covenant was made.

Generations later in the New Testament, Jesus explained to His followers a simple principle of loyalty: no one can serve two masters.

> *No one can be a slave of two masters, since either he will hate one and love the other, or be devoted to one and despise the other. You cannot be slaves of God and of money. (Matthew 6:24)*

In this passage, He was referring to money, but the principle remains—we must choose who or what we will follow, honor, and give respect to. Anything or any person can become an idol if it becomes a source of worship. In Exodus 20, the first two commandments focus on the priority we are to give the Lord:

> *Do not have other gods besides Me.*
>
> *Do not make an idol for yourself, whether in the shape of anything in the heavens above or on the earth below or in the waters under the earth.*
>
> *You must not bow down to them or worship them; for I, the Lord your God, am a jealous God, punishing the children for the fathers' sin, to the third and fourth generations of those who hate Me, but showing faithful love to a thousand generations of those who love Me and keep My commands. (Exodus 20:3–6)*

The Lord will not accept second billing to anyone, nor should He. As our Creator, we owe Him *everything*. As our Savior, we owe Him *everything*. And as the Holy Spirit continually guiding us, we owe Him *everything*. This is the basis for the Christian faith. If we can't understand or won't accept this, we have no faith and therefore, no hope for eternity. It is only through belief in Christ and the life He gave for us that we can spend eternity in heaven.

By now, it should be clear that grey areas live and thrive in our false realities and fantasies. They are created to appease and justify our own opinions and sinful nature and are not healthy for us physically or spiritually. We were created for more, in this life and the life to come; but we get to decide. Do we want to follow Jesus, trust His word, and walk in freedom from our guilt and shame? For me, I can't help but choose Jesus, because any other belief system ignores our created purpose and empowers the deception of grey to get in the way.

NOTES

All scripture references from the Holy Bible: Holman Christian Standard Version. 2009. Nashville: Holman Bible Publishers. As found in the Logos Bible study software program.

1. Torahclass.com
Old Testament Studies, Lesson 2 Chapter 1

2. Torahclass.com
Old Testament Studies, Lesson 2 Chapter 1

3. Torahclass.com
Old Testament Studies, Lesson 2 Chapter 1

4. https://www.merriam-webster.com/dictionary/separate

5. 5 Torahclass.com
Old Testament Studies, Lesson 2 Chapter 1

ABOUT THE AUTHOR

Blake Lawhon is a first-time author, husband and father of four, who resides in the small town of Mineral Wells, Texas. Though most of his professional career has been in sales and management, Blake has been in church leadership for twenty-five years. In his spare time, Blake enjoys watching college football and playing games with his family. He also engages regularly in one-on- one conversations with others regarding the contents of scripture. He is a dedicated follower of Jesus Christ and has written this book in obedience to his calling.